Read & Respond

Ages 7–11

C000161128

War G...

Teachers' notes ....

Guided reading

Teachers' notes 4

Shared reading

Teachers' notes 7
Photocopiable extracts........................... 8

Plot, character and setting

Activity notes 11
Photocopiable activities 15

Talk about it

Activity notes 19
Photocopiable activities 22

Get writing

Activity notes 25
Photocopiable activities 28

Assessment

Teachers' notes and activity 31
Photocopiable activity 32

Read & Respond

Ages
7–11

Author: Jillian Powell

Commissioning Editor: Rachel Mackinnon

Editor: Sarah Snashall

Assistant Editor: Kim Vernon

Series Designer: Anna Oliwa

Designer: Dan Prescott

Text © 2011 Jillian Powell © 2011 Scholastic Ltd

Designed using Adobe InDesign

Published by Scholastic Ltd,
Book End, Range Road, Witney,
Oxfordshire OX29 0YD
www.scholastic.co.uk

Printed by Bell & Bain
1 2 3 4 5 6 7 8 9   1 2 3 4 5 6 7 8 9 0

British Library Cataloguing-in-Publication Data
A catalogue record for this book is available from the British Library.

ISBN 978-1407-12707-1

The right of Jillian Powell to be identified as the author of this work has been asserted by her in accordance with the Copyright, Designs and Patents Act 1988.

Extracts from the Primary National Strategy's Primary Framework for Literacy (2006) nationalstrategies.standards.dcsf.gov.uk/primary/primaryframework/literacyframework © Crown copyright. Reproduced under the terms of the Click Use Licence.

All rights reserved. This book is sold subject to the condition that it shall not, by way of trade or otherwise, be lent, hired out or otherwise circulated without the publisher's prior consent in any form of binding or cover other than that in which it is published and without a similar condition, including this condition, being imposed upon the subsequent purchaser.

No part of this publication may be reproduced, stored in a retrieval system, or transmitted, in any form or by any means, electronic, mechanical, photocopying, recording or otherwise, without the prior permission of the publisher. This book remains copyright, although permission is granted to copy pages where indicated for classroom distribution and use only in the school which has purchased the book, or by the teacher who has purchased the book, and in accordance with the CLA licensing agreement. Photocopying permission is given only for purchasers and not for borrowers of books from any lending service.

Acknowledgements
The publishers gratefully acknowledge permission to reproduce the following copyright material: **Anova Books** for the use of text and illustrations from *War Game* by Michael Foreman. Text and illustrations © 1989, Michael Foreman. (1989, Pavilion Books). **Penguin Group Ltd** for the use of the book cover from *War Game* by Michael Foreman. (1989, Pavilion Books). Every effort has been made to trace copyright holders for the works reproduced in this book, and the publishers apologise for any inadvertent omissions.

War Game

About the book

War Game is the first of a trilogy of books inspired by the author's experience of the Second World War and his family's experiences of the First and Second World Wars. In a starkly told and fast-moving narrative, the author relates the story of four young boys from rural Suffolk who enlist to fight in the trenches of the First World War (1914–18). Drawing on the experiences of his own uncles who died as young men in the Great War, and authentic reports from the Western Front, he describes the boys' journey from the English countryside to the hellish mud of the trenches, and from patriotic excitement, to a dawning realisation of the horrors of trench warfare. The climax of the story, which gives the novel its ironic title, is based on the impromptu football matches that broke out along the Front during the spontaneous Christmas Truce of 1914. Its theme of common humanity in the face of conflict and disaster conveys the same anti-war message expressed by the author in his first children's book, *The General*, published in 1961. The succinct and unembellished narrative style of the novel is complemented by the use of authentic war-time posters and materials, and the author's own gentle and atmospheric watercolours that capture grim reality, as well as moments of magic and fun.

About the author

Michael Foreman was born in Suffolk in 1938 and grew up near Lowestoft in a village where his mother ran the newsagent's. He went to Lowestoft Art School at the age of 15 and then onto St Martin's School of Art and the Royal College of Art. His first children's book, *The General*, was published when he was still a student. Since then he has published over 300 books for adults and children, as well as working on magazines, animated films and television commercials.

He described growing up during the Second World War and its aftermath in his memoir, *War Boy: A Country Childhood* (1989). In it, he relates his early memories of air raids and firebombs, and time spent exploring bombsites and newly

liberated beaches in the years after the war. Alongside the narrative, he uses a combination of his own watercolours and pen and ink drawings as well as photographs and advertisements from the time.

He has illustrated books by many major authors, including the work of his good friend Michael Morpurgo, as well as writing and illustrating his own books. He is a keen traveller and sketches prolifically, collecting ideas and materials for his books. His home is now St Ives on the Cornish coast, and he says that football is the only hobby he has time for.

Facts and figures
War Game
First published 1989
Winner of Smarties Book Prize, 1993
Other awards:
Victoria & Albert Museum Francis Williams Prize, 1972 for *Horatio*
Victoria & Albert Museum Francis Williams Prize, 1977 for *Monkey and the Three Wizards*
The Kate Greenaway Medal, 1982 for *Long Neck and Thunder Foot*
The Kate Greenaway Medal, 1989 for *War Boy: A Country Childhood*

Guided reading

First reading

The first reading should be used to familiarise the children with the story and introduce the key themes and ideas.

Expectations

Look together at the cover of the book. Ask the children what they think the story is about – what do they learn from the title and illustration? Suggest different interpretations of the title – a game played by soldiers during a war or an ironic reference to war itself as a game. Now turn to the back cover and read the blurb together. Elicit that the background is the First World War (1914–18) and explain that it was fought between Britain and her Allies (France and Russia) and Germany and her allies (Austria-Hungary and Turkey). Ensure that they differentiate between the First World War and the Second World War (1939–45). Tell them that it was also called the Great War, and the 'war to end all wars' as it was so catastrophic. Explain how millions of young men died in the war – some villages losing a whole generation of young men. Read the dedication on the title page, noting the ages of the soldiers, their names and the reference to Christmas.

The Call to Arms

Look together at the *Punch* advertisement opposite the title page. Ensure that the children understand the message being promoted: that playing on a football field earns a wage, but going to a field of war is the only way to win true honour.

Read to where the young men walk back to the village. Ask them to summarise the setting and period. (Rural Suffolk when the First World War was just starting.) *How do the young men see the war?* (As something that will be an exciting adventure and be over by Christmas.) Look at the postbox flyer and read the headings. Discuss what the 'Call to Arms' was – a call for volunteers to join up and go and fight the enemy.

Read on to the end of the first chapter. Ask the children to summarise why the men are being called to fight. *What are they trying to prevent?* (The German Emperor sending his army to seize territory from other countries in Europe.) Look again at the posters and emphasise that these are genuine posters that were used at the time. Do the children think the posters give an honest view of the experience of war?

Discuss the concept of 'patriotism' – the love for a country, and wanting to protect it and fight for it. Ask: *What else inspires the young men to want to join up?* (The desire for travel and excitement; to show that they're men.) Explain that in the early 20th century, there was no air travel, and many people had never travelled outside their own county, let alone country.

Continue reading the next chapter 'The adventure', pausing to look at the illustrations and what they suggest – the patriotic fervour of the crowds, the excitement of a big ship leaving the harbour. Ask the children why they think the young men join up so quickly – do they really know what they are signing up for or do they just get caught up in the excitement of it all?

Trench warfare

Read 'To the Front', pausing to mark the sudden change of mood in the narrative, reflected in the illustrations that first show jolly crowds cheering the marching soldiers on, and then a much darker scene as refugees trudge through a war-torn landscape. Point out the non-fiction style in this section of the book.

Explain the principles of 'trench warfare', in which opposing armies face each other across a patch of land known as No Man's Land, firing shells, mortars and machine guns. When ordered they need to go 'over the top' of their trenches and attempt to move their troops further forward and take possession of more land. Pause to look at the poster of the dog and ensure that the children understand what 'sentries' are – guard or watch dogs that warn of approaching danger. Tell the children that as well as dogs, pigeons were used in the war as messengers and horses were used as transport for men, weapons and supplies – an estimated 8 million war horses were killed.

Read 'No Man's Land' up to *The enemy trenches were so close...* Discuss how different the reality of the war is from what the boys expected. Ask the children to summarise the conditions the soldiers are living in: rain, mud and squalor. Tell the children that the mud was so bad, that sometimes the men's feet were never dry and became infected with a fungal infection called 'trench foot', which could result in the foot being amputated.

The Christmas Truce

Read up to *But Boxing Day passed without...* Ask the children to explain what happens. (The enemy armies begin singing carols to each other from their trenches, then get together to bury the dead, exchange gifts and finally play a friendly game of football.) Why do the children think the officers would be angry? (They are concerned that the men will stop seeing the Germans as enemies and will lose the will to fight.) Explain that all this is based on real events – even down to the details of the gifts exchanged and the German barber giving haircuts or shaves to English soldiers. Tell them that on Christmas Day, 1914, a number of spontaneous football matches really did break out along the Western Front, much to the consternation of the officers.

Over the top

Continue reading to the end. Pause to ask whether the children understand the German words *wasser* (water) and *kinder* (children). Ask them to explain how the author uses a metaphor to describe the boys going 'over the top' of the parapet into No Man's Land (as if it were a football game). What do they think happens to the young men? (They are all killed by enemy gunfire.) Pause at the end of the first reading to ask the children to describe how the story has made them feel.

Second reading

Use subsequent readings to explore in more depth some of the key ideas and themes in the novel. As they already know the storyline, they can now concentrate on different aspects, such as themes, text features and illustrations.

Illustrations and text features

Focus on the two types of illustration: the author's watercolours, which depict events described in the text, and the contemporary print media, such as advertisements, posters and flyers. Ask: *How does each contribute to the narrative?* (The watercolours help us visualise the scenes described; the contemporary materials make the story 'real'.)

Fiction or non-fiction

Look at the use of italicised captions that give facts about the war. Discuss how this is usually a non-fiction feature. Read a selection of captions and ask the children what they contribute to the story. They are written in the factual style, reminding us that this story, although written about a fictional group of friends, is based on historical facts about the First World War. Encourage the children to identify other non-fiction threads such as the author's dedication on the first page to his uncles (who share the names of the characters in the book), the contemporary war posters and advertisements.

Structure ~ a journey

Read the first two chapters together. Ask the children to summarise the mood at the beginning of the story. (Excitement, anticipation.) Point out that this is the start of a journey for the young men. Can the children suggest more than one way in which the story relates a journey? (Literally from England to France, and also emotionally from excitement to horror.)

Read on until the bus arrives at the trenches.

Guided reading

Ask the children to list what changes as the men journey through France – the weather, the landscape, the demeanour of the people. Ask: *What is the mood of the men as they travel on the London bus?* (Optimistic, still keen to enjoy the adventure.) Highlight the fact that none of them has ever been on a London bus, again showing how little they have travelled, and why this would have been such an adventure. Continue until the part where it mentions the rats disappearing. Track how the young men's emotions change as the reality of war becomes apparent.

Consider the significance of the rats leaving the trenches and ask the children whether they have heard or read stories about animals being sensitive to approaching danger: for example, there were reports of animals fleeing to higher ground before the Asian tsunami of 2004. Ensure that the children understand the meaning of 'heavy shelling' – the use of explosive shells fired from field guns. Explain that many soldiers had to be sent home from war with 'shell shock', a disabling psychological trauma caused by the incessant shell blasts they experienced on the frontline.

Full circle

Continue to where the Germans attack again after the truce. Ask the children to list all the things that lighten the mood during the truce. (The snow, the carols, the sparrows and skylarks, football game, gifts.) Read on to the end of the novel. Focus on the way the action when the men go over the top is described in terms of a football match. Ask the children how the story comes full circle. (It begins with a football game, and ends with an imaginary game as the young men run into the gunfire.) Ensure that the children understand that the ending implies rather than states that the young men all die, reminding them of the author's uncles in the dedication. Do they think that the ending is effective and, if so, why? Suggest that the football metaphor is fitting in that it captures the youthful enthusiasm they carried to war, which ends so tragically. Similarly poignant treatments can be seen in films and television series such as the final episode of the comedy *Blackadder Goes Forth*, where the pals go 'over the top' to their death, and their running figures fade into the Flanders poppies that grew up where they died.

Shared reading

Extract 1

- Establish where the soldiers are marching. (Across Northern France towards the Front.) Circle the word *Front* and ask them to explain what or where it was (the line along which the enemy troops were fighting). Ask: *Who is giving the soldiers gifts and why?* (The French people, because these soldiers are coming to fight the enemy German army, which is occupying part of France.)
- Discuss any vocabulary that might be unfamiliar (*babel, shunted, salvage, artillery*). Explain the story of the Tower of Babel and discuss how this quickly allows Michael Foreman to create a sense of many people talking at once in different languages.
- Pick out all the facts we learn about the war. (The use of horses and mules, trenches and wire, artillery, and so on.)
- Together, summarise what has happened to the people the soldiers see. (They have lost their homes and farms because of the war.) Gather some words to describe the landscape the soldiers are approaching. (Bleak, destroyed, shattered.)

Extract 2

- Establish where Will and Freddie are. (In a trench along the Front, looking out over No Man's Land.) Circle the words *No Man's Land* and ask the children to explain where this was. (The area between the opposing front lines.)
- Discuss the meaning of *sentries, fire-step* and *parapet*. (Sentries were look-outs; they stood on a step built inside the trench for firing from behind the parapet, the front side of the trench which would be lined with sandbags.) Ask: *Why do the boys peer so cautiously over the top?* (The enemy might fire at them.)
- Focus on the description of the landscape. Circle the word *seeped* and challenge the children to suggest a word or phrase that could replace it. (Passed slowly, gradually.) Ask: *Which sentence is incomplete here?* (A landscape as flat as the fields of home.) *Which landscape does it refer to?* (The landscape of Suffolk in East Anglia.)
- Pick out the evocative verbs used for describing the flares. (*Arced, spiralled.*)
- Make the link between Freddie's comment on the enemy lines and the title of the novel. (He sees it in football terms.)

Extract 3

- Ask the children what makes this Christmas Eve special? (The snow, the carols, the ceasefire.)
- Can the children explain the phrase *'Stood To'*? (When the men went on watch on the fire-step an hour before dawn, when the enemy might be expected to attack.)
- Challenge them to find examples of similes (*like bedraggled moles, like tinsel, like a Star of Bethlehem*) and a metaphor (*the clock of death*).

Ask: *In what ways are the men like moles?* (They are living in underground tunnels or trenches, in the mud and darkness.)
- Ask: *How does the frost transform the landscape?* (It hides the horror of the wires and dead bodies.) Can the children explain the reference to a Star of Bethlehem? (An exploding shell in the distance looks like the star that led the Wise Men to the stable.)

Extract 1

To the Front

The soldiers finally arrived at a small station that had grown into a vast supply depot. Trains and trucks were being shunted and unloaded. Mountains of stores, horse lines and mule lines were everywhere, and there was a babel of shouted commands.

Then at last they were off the trains and marching. Will felt good to be out in the fresh air and swinging along with his mates. Marching through villages and towns, the troops were cheered all the way. Flowers, fruit and bread were pressed into their arms. It seemed like a pretty good war so far, even though it had begun to rain and the long dry summer was over.

Then things began to change. The roads became crowded with people moving back from the Front. The whole population seemed to be on the move. Families carried their children and pushed prams loaded with whatever they could salvage from their lives. No more cheering crowds. These people had seen war. Their homes had been blown to bits, their farms criss-crossed by armies, trenches, wire, and pock-marked by a million artillery shells. Will could hear the almost continuous sound of shellfire in the distance.

They passed wagons full of wounded soldiers on their way back to England, and long lines of exhausted ragged troops sitting in the mud, rain and gathering darkness before being ordered back into the action.

Extract 2

No Man's Land

Will and Freddie were the first to be posted as sentries on their little section, and, cautiously, they stood up on the fire-step. They peered over the parapet into No Man's Land. They could just see their own first line of wire and random humps and bumps in an otherwise flat landscape that seeped rapidly into darkness. A landscape as flat as the fields of home.

Then a flare arced and spiralled slowly from the sky. Will and Freddie could see that the humps and bumps were men. Dead men. Some of them, who had cut their trousers into shorts during the hot weather, looked like fallen schoolboys.

Before the flare faded, Will and Freddie saw more lines of wire and, beyond No Man's Land, the front line of German trenches.

'Less than a goal-kick away,' whispered Freddie.

Text and illustrations © 1989, Michael Foreman.

Extract 3

No Man's Land

Will, Freddie, Lacey and Billy stayed together as much as possible and lived like bedraggled moles in a world of mud, attack and counter-attack.

The weather, still wet, grew steadily colder. Then, one night, as the lads returned to the Front after a few days' rest, the rain stopped and it grew bitterly cold.

That night they were relieving a Scottish regiment, and as the Scots left the Line, the Germans shouted Christmas wishes to them.

Then tiny lights appeared in the German trenches. As far as the eye could see, Christmas trees were flickering along the parapet of the German lines.

It was Christmas Eve.

A single German voice began to sing 'Silent Night'. It was joined by many others.

The British replied with 'The First Noel' to applause from the Germans. And so it went on, turn and turn about. Then both front lines sang 'O Come All Ye Faithful'.

It was a beautiful moonlit night. Occasionally a star shell hung like a Star of Bethlehem.

At dawn, when the British were all 'Stood To' on the fire-step, they saw a world white with frost. The few shattered trees that remained were white. Lines of wire glinted like tinsel. The humps of dead in No Man's Land were like toppled snowmen.

After the singing of the night, the Christmas dawn was strangely quiet. The clock of death had stopped ticking.

Plot, character and setting

Expectations

> **Objective:** To identify and make notes of the main points of sections of texts.
> **What you need:** Copies of *War Game,* individual whiteboards and pens.

What to do
- Look together at the chapter titles used in the early part of the book ('The Kick-Off', 'The Adventure', 'To the Front' and 'No Man's Land'). Discuss what expectations each title raises, pointing out how 'The Kick-Off', like the title *War Game,* could have two meanings: the start of a football game, and also the start of the boys' adventure going to war.
- Point out that after 'No Man's Land', there are no chapter titles. Arrange the children in pairs and challenge them to think of some of their own chapter titles for this section of the book, and

to capture their favourite on their whiteboards, noting the page number. (For example, page 57 'The Truce'; page 84 'Over the Top'.)
- Together, share the chapter titles. Discuss what expectations they raise about the section of story. (They might indicate where the men are, what they are doing, or how they are feeling.)

> **Differentiation**
> **For older/more confident learners:** Challenge pairs to write brief chapter summaries to go with their titles, for example 'The Truce': Christmas brings about a ceasefire between enemy forces.
> **For younger/less confident learners:** Provide key page references to support these children, and discuss the gist of the action in each section with them.

The Great War facts

> **Objective:** To use knowledge of different organisational features of texts to find information effectively.
> **What you need:** Copies of *War Game,* photocopiable page 15.
> **Cross-curricular link:** History.

What to do
- Encourage the children to think about key facts about the First World War that they have learned from *War Game* (trench warfare, weapons used, and so on).
- Hand out photocopiable page 15 to small groups. Tell the groups to complete the sheets using information taken from the novel. They should refer back to the text to help them.
- When they have completed their sheets, challenge them to think of three questions about the war that will need research outside of *War*

Game, for example:
  - *How long did the war last?*
  - *How many people were killed?*
  - *What finally brought the war to an end?*
- Together, discuss the answers to the questions on the photocopiable sheet. Capture on the board the new questions the children have asked and discuss where they might search to find out answers.
- Provide time for the children to research the answers to the new questions.

> **Differentiation**
> **For older/more confident learners:** Steer the children to more complicated questions for their research.
> **For younger/less confident learners:** Steer the children towards questions that are straightforward to answer.

Plot, character and setting

A brief history

> **Objective:** To interrogate texts to deepen and clarify understanding and response.
> **What you need:** Copies of *War Game*.
> **Cross-curricular link:** History.

What to do
- Elicit that in *War Game* the author has shaped historical fact into a fictional storyline.
- Recap that a novel needs a beginning, a middle and an ending. On the left-hand side of the board, write 'Beginning', 'Middle' and 'Ending' and ask the children to suggest content from the novel to go under each heading (for example, 'joining up', 'in the trenches', 'going over the top').
- Ask the children to think of themes that recur through all phases of the novel (friendship, football, weather/seasons, mood, landscape). List these on the right-hand side of the board.

- As a shared activity, discuss how each theme appears at different stages of the novel: for example, the football match in Suffolk at the beginning, the match between enemies in the middle, and the imaginary match in Will's head at the end. Add these details under 'Beginning', 'Middle' and 'End' to highlight how the themes are covered across the story.

> **Differentiation**
> **For older/more confident learners:** Encourage the children to explore further how landscape or the seasons or friendship appear in the story.
> **For younger/less confident learners:** Help the children to locate the theme of football for each heading. Encourage them to look at the illustrations as well.

Plot shuffle

> **Objective:** To identify and summarise evidence from a text.
> **What you need:** Copies of *War Game*, photocopiable page 16, chapter titles created in 'Expectations', scissors.

What to do
- Hand out photocopiable page 16 and ask the children to note where each element appeared in the story. Get them to cut out and rearrange the boxes in plot order.
- Ask the children to indicate which box takes place in which chapter using both Michael Foreman's chapter headings and their own chapter headings from 'Expectations'.
- Suggest that although the storyline is chronological, it could perhaps be told another way, for example, using flashbacks. Challenge the children to rearrange the plot elements to tell the story using one or two flashbacks (for

example, the soldiers might recall the Suffolk football match or signing up at the Town Hall when they are in the trenches).
- Discuss these as a class, and how flashbacks could be used if the novel was being adapted as a film.
- Challenge the children to choose an early episode from the story and write a short brief showing when and how it could appear later in the plot as a flashback.

> **Differentiation**
> **For older/more confident learners:** Ask the children to capture the emotions of the soldier during the flashback.
> **For younger/less confident learners:** Ask the children to write a brief for Will and Freddie remembering signing up at the Town Hall while on sentry duty.

Plot, character and setting

Pals in war

Objective: To infer characters' feelings in fiction.
What you need: Copies of *War Game*, photocopiable page 17, individual whiteboards and pens.
Cross-curricular link: PSHE.

What to do

● Re-read the first two chapters. Ask the children to name the main characters in the story and summarise some key facts we learn about them. (They live in rural Suffolk, play in a village football team together, sign up together, and so on.)

● Explain that, in the First World War, many groups of friends enlisted together – sometimes a whole football team. They formed 'Pals' or 'Chums' Battalions. Discuss how Will and his friends sign up like this, with great enthusiasm.

● Ask: *How do the young men's feelings about the war change when they reach the Front?* (They realise the horror of trench warfare when they see all the dead bodies and destruction.)

● Hand out photocopiable page 17 and ask the children to work in pairs to fill it in. Explain they need to scan the novel to find events that trigger each emotion in Will and his pals.

Differentiation
For older/more confident learners: Challenge pairs to use the completed photocopiable sheet to design a mind map showing the feelings experienced by Wills and his pals in the war.
For younger/less confident learners: Provide page numbers to help the children locate the events.

Soldiers' senses

Objective: To empathise with characters.
What you need: Copies of *War Game*, individual whiteboards and pens.
Cross-curricular link: History.

What to do

● Tell the children that, in this lesson, they are going to think about what it was really like for the soldiers in the trenches, not just the sights they saw, but the sounds, smells and feel of warfare.

● Write headings for each of the five senses on the board: sights, sounds, smells, feel or touch, taste.

● Next, ask for anything they can recall to go under these headings, for example, the sight of flares arcing across the sky, or the sound of shells exploding.

● Tell the children to work in pairs and scan through the trench descriptions from *Then they were in the trenches…* to *Will, Freddie, Lacey and Billy stayed together…* They should use their whiteboards to jot down all the examples they can find of sights, sounds, smells, and so on.

● When they have finished, bring the class back together and ask for contributions from pairs, to fill in columns under the headings on the board.

Differentiation
For older/more confident learners: Ask the pairs to write a descriptive sentence for each sense, expanding one of the examples they located: for example, they might describe the smell of breakfast wafting from the enemy trenches, or the sound of machine-gun fire.
For younger/less confident learners: Ask pairs to focus on capturing sights and sounds in the book.

Plot, character and setting

War diaries

> **Objective:** To use settings and characterisation to engage readers' interest.
> **What you need:** Copies of *War Game*, individual whiteboards and pens.
> **Cross-curricular link:** History.

What to do

● Tell the children that they are going to draft a diary entry that Will might have written while he was in the trenches describing the daily routine.

● Read together the section on trench life, from *The newcomers quickly learned the routine…* to *Sometimes the rats would suddenly disappear…* As a shared activity, work through the text highlighting any salient facts the diary entry could include. (When the soldiers are woken, the temperature, the infested trenches, the biscuits.)

● Revise some key features of diaries: they are written in the first person, they can be informal, even note-style in form, chronological recount.

● Discuss different ways of beginning Will's diary entry, writing suggestions on the board, for example: 'Freezing cold this morning. Woken at what seemed like the middle of the night…'.

● Tell the children to read on to *The enemy trenches were so close that…*, scanning the text for facts about the daily routine, then allow them time to draft and edit Will's diary entry for a typical day.

● Invite volunteers to read out their entry and invite constructive feedback.

> **Differentiation**
> **For older/more confident learners:** The children can draft another diary entry describing an episode chosen from the novel, for example, their journey across France or Christmas Day.
> **For younger/less confident learners:** Scan the whole section of text as a shared activity, noting down salient facts on the board for children to use in their diary entries.

Simply similes

> **Objective:** To explain how writers use figurative and expressive language to create images and atmosphere.
> **What you need:** Copies of *War Game*, individual whiteboards and pens, photocopiable page 18.

What to do

● Tell the children that, in this lesson, they are going to focus on descriptive writing that creates the setting and atmosphere in the novel, in particular the use of similes.

● Briefly revise what a simile is, and what it is used for. (To enhance descriptive writing, help readers to visualise something by comparing it to something else.) Write an example from the novel on the flipchart, for example *Lines of wire glinted like tinsel.* Discuss what this evokes. (Frost sparkling on wire like Christmas decorations; a respite from the horror of war.)

● Arrange the class into pairs. Challenge them to scan the novel to find similes and note them on their whiteboards. They should discuss together what each evokes.

● Hand out photocopiable page 18 and ask pairs to fill it in.

● Bring the class back together and invite pairs to share their reactions to the similes in the book and their own similes, discussing which work best and why.

> **Differentiation**
> **For older/more confident learners:** Challenge children to invent some more similes describing things or places in the novel.
> **For younger/less confident learners:** Provide pairs with a frame for their similes by first describing what the thing is like and then thinking what else is like that. Help them to use their thoughts to create the simile.

Plot, character and setting

SECTION
4

The Great War facts

● Use *War Game* to find the answers to these questions about the First World War. Write three new questions about the war on the back of this page.

Who fought whom in the First World War and why?

_____

_____

When did the war start?

_____

What did people think it would be like?

_____

_____

Where was 'The Front'?

_____

_____

What weapons were used?

_____

_____

How were animals used in the war?

_____

_____

Describe some of the horrors that soldiers faced.

_____

_____

_____

_____

Illustrations © 1989, Michael Foreman.

SECTION
4

Plot shuffle

- Explain how each of the following features in the storyline.
- Cut out the boxes and stick them in the order they appear in the book.

A barber	Fifty sparrows
A water bottle	A carol
The Town Hall	Bell tents
A bus journey	A goal

SCHOLASTIC
www.scholastic.co.uk

Pals in war

● Write down an event or situation that makes Will and his pals feel:

Disappointed and foolish

_____

_____

Excited

_____

_____

Shocked

_____

_____

Cheered up

_____

_____

Proud

_____

_____

Cautious

_____

_____

_____

Illustrations © 1989, Michael Foreman.

SECTION
4

Simply similes

● Explain what is being described in these similes:

'like bedraggled moles'

_____

'like fallen schoolboys'

_____

'like a Star of Bethlehem'

_____

'like toppled snowmen'

_____

● Write a sentence that includes a simile describing each of the following:

The dead trees

_____

The mud

_____

The pistol flares

_____

Shell craters

_____

■SCHOLASTIC
www.scholastic.co.uk

Talk about it

Propaganda!

> **Objective:** To offer reasons and evidence for their views, considering alternative opinions.
> **What you need:** Copies of *War Game*, individual whiteboards and pens.
> **Cross-curricular links:** History, citizenship, ICT.

What to do

● Look together at the 'Britons' poster. Explain that this famous poster from 1914 shows the Secretary of State for War, Lord Kitchener, appealing for recruits like Will and his pals to enlist. Discuss its impact: the pointing finger, and direct address; 'YOU' in large type, the patriotic words taken from the national anthem (God Save the King).

● Write 'PROPAGANDA' on the board and ask the children whether they can explain what it means. (Using media to try to influence the attitudes or actions of a community.) Explain that propaganda was widely used through the media of the time (posters, newspapers) to encourage people to join in the war effort.

● Arrange the class into small groups and assign each a poster from the novel to discuss: *What is its message? Who is it aimed at? How effective is it as propaganda and why?* They should note ideas on their whiteboards, then prepare a short presentation about the poster.

● Share the presentations as a class, encouraging constructive feedback.

> **Differentiation**
> **For older/more confident learners:** Groups could use ICT, for example, presentation software to present their materials to the class.
> **For younger/less confident learners:** Provide a template with questions for groups to answer about their poster to prompt discussion: *What is the poster's message? Who is it aimed at? What is the intended effect of images or words? How effective is it?*

Officers and men

> **Objective:** To create roles showing how behaviour can be interpreted from different viewpoints.
> **What you need:** Copies of *War Game*.
> **Cross-curricular link:** Drama.

What to do

● Together, re-read the passage describing the impromptu football match and its aftermath. Ask the children to explain why the officers in command might be alarmed by it. (The soldiers might stop seeing the Germans as 'the enemy'.)

● Arrange the children into small groups to improvise a short drama scene in which officers at army headquarters react to news of the match and the Christmas Truce. They should imagine that the officers summon Will and Freddie and ask them to explain what happened.

● Before they begin, ask them to discuss how the men are feeling (cheered up, exuberant) and how the officers may be feeling (angry and worried). How do the children think the officers might behave towards the men? (Angry, intimidating, threatening.)

● Observe groups as they improvise their scenes, and invite one or two to perform for the class. Encourage constructive feedback and criticism.

● Tell the children that later in the war, men who 'fraternised' with the enemy were sometimes shot.

> **Differentiation**
> **For older/more confident learners:** Groups could improvise another scene with the German soldiers talking among themselves after the truce.
> **For younger/less confident learners:** Discuss with the children how the men and the officers are feeling, and how they would behave towards each other, before leaving the children to improvise.

Talk about it

Friendly matches

> **Objective:** To actively include and respond to all members of the group.
> **What you need:** Copies of *War Game*, individual whiteboards and pens.
> **Cross-curricular link:** PSHE.

What to do

● Focus on the theme of football in the novel. Ask: *How does the theme recur?* (The opening football match, the match against the Germans, the imaginary match at the end, Freddie measuring No Man's Land as *less than a goal-kick away*.)

● Revisit the irony of the novel's title. (Contrasting the game that takes place with the 'game' of war.) Ask the children how football and war are opposites in the novel (War divides peoples; football brings them together). Tell them about recent football matches that have brought temporary truces between Israelis and Palestinians.

● Arrange the class into small groups and ask them to create a list on their whiteboards of all the ways in which football can be used to bring communities or peoples together. (Matches to bring together different gangs or ethnic groups in local communities, friendly matches between work employees, charity matches.)

● Remind the children of the rules of group discussion.

● When they have finished, bring the class together to discuss ideas for how football (or sport in general) can be a force for good in the community.

> **Differentiation**
> **For older/more confident learners:** Let groups discuss the risk of football causing divisions. (Fighting between supporters, racism in football.)
> **For younger/less confident learners:** Provide the children with some prompt words: communities, divisions, conflict, sharing.

For King and Country

> **Objective:** To interrogate texts to deepen and clarify understanding and response.
> **What you need:** Copies of *War Game*, photocopiable page 22.
> **Cross-curricular links:** History, citizenship.

What to do

● Ask: *What does 'Patriotism' mean?* Capture a range of correct answers on the board. (Singing patriotic songs, national anthems, flag waving.) Ask: *What might patriotic behaviour be?* Encourage them to think about volunteering, voting, good citizenship as well as military service, and so on.

● Look together at the 'A Call to Arms' and 'Women of Britain Say – "Go"' posters and the newspaper advertisements in 'The Adventure' chapter. Discuss how they try to make people act patriotically (encouraging women to wear badges to show relatives have joined up, urging young men to fight for their country).

● Hand out photocopiable page 22. Ask the children to work in pairs to complete it and then bring the class back together to share their ideas.

● As a class, discuss how children might express patriotism today, such as displaying national flags during World Cup tournaments, or attending events to welcome home soldiers or honour soldiers who have died for their country.

● Broaden the discussion to ask if and how patriotism might sometimes lead to less positive emotions, such as nationalism or even racism.

> **Differentiation**
> **For older/more confident learners:** Encourage children to think further about their ideas, for example, can they suggest ways children could have raised funds to help in the war effort?
> **For younger/less confident learners:** Let children complete the first part of the photocopiable sheet in pairs, then discuss the second part as a class.

Talk about it

War ~ then and now

Objective: To debate moral dilemmas portrayed in texts.
What you need: Copies of *War Game*, photocopiable page 23.
Cross-curricular link: Citizenship.

What to do

● Briefly discuss what the children know about recent and current wars. Capture the children's comments on the board. Encourage them to volunteer experiences of brothers or fathers in the army, being sensitive to individual circumstances.
● The First World War took place a century ago; introduce the subject of war today. Ask: *How is war today similar or different from the First World War?* (Today, joining the Army is a career choice; Will and his friends were recruited as volunteers but in 1916 conscription was introduced. Then, war was portrayed as noble and exciting; today we are more honest about the horror of war.)

● Hand out photocopiable page 23 and organise the children to work in pairs. If possible, provide access to the internet. Encourage the children to discuss the answers and listen to each other as they talk, before deciding what to write.
● Bring the class back together and discuss how similar or different they think the experiences of today's soldiers are from those of Will and his friends.

Differentiation
For older/more confident learners: Let pairs discuss possible storylines for a novel using today's wars – for example, young men who come back from war with life-changing injuries, or who lose close comrades.
For younger/less confident learners: Let pairs focus on discussing what makes soldiers want to join up today, and how they are similar or different from the young men who signed up to fight in the First World War.

War report

Objective: To use drama strategies to explore stories or issues.
What you need: Copies of *War Game*, photocopiable sheet 24, if possible, images of contemporary newspaper reports.
Cross-curricular links: Drama, citizenship, history.

What to do

● Read together the chapter 'The Adventure'. Ask the children how all the excitement might have been reported at the time – explain that there was no television or radio then. Elicit that the coverage would have been in newspapers (if possible, show images of newspapers reporting the war), news films shown in the cinema and photographs.
● Tell the children that they are going to improvise a television news report about the soldiers going off to war. Arrange them into small groups and ask them to scan through the chapter

and decide together what the reporter might show and whom he or she might interview.
● Hand out photocopiable page 24 and explain that they should use this to plan their report. Remind them to listen to each other and build on each other's ideas.
● Give groups time to allocate parts and improvise their drama using their plans.
● Share the different reports.

Differentiation
For older/more confident learners: Encourage groups to record their news reports using video cameras.
For younger/less confident learners: Provide the children with a list of people to choose from to interview (a recruit, a mother, the captain of the ship, a younger brother, a veteran, and so on) and provide some questions to ask to allow these children to focus on their answers.

Talk about it

For King and Country

● Explain how the army encouraged these groups to be 'Patriots' during the war.

Women

Shopkeepers

Young Men

Veterans

● Suggest three ways that children of the time could be 'Patriots':

1. _____

2. _____

3. _____

Talk about it

War – then and now

● Discuss the following aspects of war, during the First World War and during conflicts today, with your partner.

	First World War	Now
Who joins up and why?		
What is the purpose of war?		
What view of war does the government hold?		
Do some people hold different views of war? If so, what?		
How do soldiers communicate with their families?		
What media coverage of the war is there?		

Talk about it

War report

- Discuss with your group how you're going to create your war report.
- Fill in this chart to help you plan what you're going to do.

Where is your reporter standing?
What scene will he or she describe?
Whom will he or she interview?
1.
2.
3.
Write down three questions he or she will ask:
1.
2.
3.

Get writing

Thomas Atkins

Objective: To identify and make notes of the main points of sections of text.
What you need: Copies of *War Game*, individual whiteboards and pens.
Cross-curricular links: History, ICT.

What to do

● Read together the text about the Duke of Wellington (just before fighting resumes). Discuss how the italicised text which features from the trench scenes onwards is different from the main text and what it contributes. (It reports facts; the main text is narrative.)
● Arrange the class into pairs and ask the children to scan the novel and note down on their whiteboards any facts about the Tommies that they learn. (For example, what they ate, the colour of their uniforms, the weapons they carried, what they received as Christmas gifts.)

● When they have finished, note all their suggestions on the board and, as a shared activity, organise them into sections as for a non-chronological report, for example, diet, uniform, weapons.
● Challenge pairs to draft a paragraph about Tommies in the factual style of the italicised text, using information from the flipchart.

Differentiation
For older/more confident learners: The children could work in pairs to research further information about the Tommies using the internet or books. They can cross-check information they find with details from the novel, and use it to extend or improve their paragraphs.
For younger/less confident learners: Provide a report frame for the children to use for their notes, using headings such as: Who were the Tommies? Uniforms, Weapons, Food, Songs, Christmas gifts.

Letters home

Objective: To write non-narrative texts using structures of different text types.
What you need: Copies of *War Game*, examples of letters written home from soldiers in the First World War if possible.
Cross-curricular link: History.

What to do

● Tell the children that the only way for soldiers to keep in touch with their families from the trenches was by post (there were no telephones, let alone text messages or emails). If possible, refer to real letters sent home from the trenches, using appropriate websites providing primary sources about the First World War.
● Tell them they are going to draft a letter that Will or one of the other boys might have written home to his parents.
● Discuss the kind of things the letter might include and note their ideas on the board. (Thanking family for the Christmas gifts, asking

how things are at home, describing the events of the Christmas Truce and how the soldiers and officers reacted.)
● Briefly revise the layout of letter writing and encourage children to include an appropriate location and date. (France, 26 December 1914.)
● Give them time to draft and improve their letters. Encourage them to refer to the novel, particularly the pages on the Christmas tree to give detail to their letter.
● Invite volunteers to read out their letter and encourage constructive feedback.

Differentiation
For older/more confident learners: Let the children write a letter sent in return from a parent or sibling.
For younger/less confident learners: Provide a frame for the letter so that the children can concentrate on content and writing in the first person.

Get writing

War news

> **Objective:** To write non-narrative text types using structures of different text types.
> **What you need:** Copies of *War Game*, images of contemporary newspapers (if possible), photocopiable page 28.
> **Cross-curricular links:** Citizenship, ICT.

What to do

● Discuss the range of media we have today: 24-hour news on the internet, mobiles and television through satellite technology. Remind the children that during the First World War people relied on print media such as posters, flyers and newspapers; there was no radio or TV coverage, although there were (silent) cinema films.

● If possible, share images of newspapers of the time and discuss how different the broadsheets look from today's highly illustrated tabloids.

● Return to the idea of propaganda in newspapers of the time. Explain that news coverage would have been carefully censored to avoid anything that might hinder the war effort (very different from today's reporting – although censorship still exists).

● Tell the children they are going to plan a news report that might be written in today's style about the Christmas Truce. They should imagine they are a reporter sent to the Front, who has witnessed the Truce and the different views on it held by soldiers and officers.

● Hand out photocopiable page 28 and ask the children to fill it in.

> **Differentiation**
> **For older/more confident learners:** Children could work on the computer to create an attractive newspaper page.
> **For younger/less confident learners:** Let children work in pairs and share their plans to draft their newspaper report.

Children of Britain

> **Objective:** To choose and combine words, images and other features for particular effects.
> **What you need:** Copies of *War Game*, photocopiable page 29.
> **Cross-curricular links:** History, art and design.

What to do

● Remind the children of the work they did for the lesson 'Propaganda!' Tell them they are now going to design their own war poster in the style of those used in the novel.

● Look together at the posters in the book. Recap some of the techniques they use: direct address, family images, appeal to duty or pride or patriotism. Point out the child included in the illustration on the 'Women of Britain Say…' poster.

● Arrange the class into pairs and provide each pair with photocopiable page 29. Tell them they should use these to plan a poster aimed at children, encouraging them to be patriots during the First World War. Discuss what the poster might convey. (Children encouraging fathers or brothers to fight, raising funds for the war effort, not wasting food, helping their mothers out at home.)

● Allow them time to fill in the sheets and then sketch out their ideas for their poster. Share posters and enjoy favourite ideas.

> **Differentiation**
> **For older/more confident learners:** Let the children use ICT to create a finished poster. They could go on to design another poster, presenting an anti-war message.
> **For younger/less confident learners:** Encourage children to share ideas with their classmates so that everyone has enough ideas to create their poster.

Get writing

War poems

> **Objective:** To show imagination through language used to create emphasis, humour, atmosphere or suspense.
> **What you need:** Copies of *War Game*, examples of poems written by First World War poets, individual whiteboards and pens.
> **Cross-curricular link:** History.

What to do

● Tell the children that many great war poets emerged during the First World War, including Wilfred Owen, Siegfried Sassoon, Edmund Blunden, and John McCrae. They were young men who had experienced the horrors of the war and their poetry told people what the war was really like for the soldiers in the trenches.

● Read as many examples of First World War poetry as possible (available on many websites), for example Wilfred Owen's 'Futility'. Invite comment and interpretations from the children.

Ask: *What is the poem about? What message does it convey?*

● Explain that they are going to try writing a poem capturing what life was like in the trenches, using information taken from the novel. (For example, the churned up mud, the constant rain or glittering frost, fingers numb with cold.)

● Allow the children time to draft, redraft and finalise their poems. Bring the class back together and invite volunteers to read their poems, discussing which work best and why.

> **Differentiation**
> **For older/more confident learners:** Challenge the children to read more war poems and draft one in the style of a favourite poet.
> **For younger/less confident learners:** Steer children towards specific parts of the novel that might lead to a poem, for example, the snow scene or the trenches.

Book club

> **Objective:** To share and compare reasons for reading preferences, extending range of books read.
> **What you need:** Copies of *War Game*, photocopiable page 30.

What to do

● Tell the children that they are going to write a review of *War Game* for a book club, to help members decide whether they want to read it.

● Ask them whether they enjoyed reading the book and, if so, why. Encourage them to cite their reasons and note them on the board.

● Ask whether any of them has read any other books by Michael Foreman and how they compare. Which did they enjoy most and why? Go on to talk about any other books about war that the children may have read, noting their authors and titles, and inviting the children to

suggest which they enjoyed most, and how they were similar or different in their treatment of the subject of war. Discuss how other fictional stories set during wartime may also be based, like *War Game*, on historical fact (*Carrie's War*, *War Horse*, *The Silver Sword*, *The Machine Gunners*).

● Hand out photocopiable page 30 and ask the children to fill it in, using their knowledge of the novel.

> **Differentiation**
> **For older/more confident learners:** Challenge children to complete a review for another book about war that they have read.
> **For younger/less confident learners:** Suggest that children discuss the book in pairs or small groups before they fill in the review sheets.

Get writing

War news

- Plan a first-page news report on the Christmas Truce and football match.

THE CHRONICLE

CHRISTMAS 1914 EDITION

Headline

Brief a photograph

Brief summary

Write quotes by two interviewees about what happened.

SCHOLASTIC
www.scholastic.co.uk

Get writing

Children of Britain

● Plan a poster to encourage children to be patriots in the First World War.

What is the aim of your poster?

_____

What words will you use on your poster?

_____

What photographs or artwork will you use?

_____

What will you add to your poster to make it appeal to children?

_____

Sketch the idea for your poster here.

[empty box]

Get writing

Book club

● Write a review of *War Game* to help members of a book club to decide whether they want to read it.

Title of book _____

Author/Illustrator _____

Subject and themes _____

_____

What messages does the story contain? _____

_____

_____

What three things have you learned about the war from the novel?

1. _____

2. _____

3. _____

How do the illustrations help to convey ideas or mood? _____

_____

_____

Would you recommend the book to others and, if so, why? _____

_____

_____

Assessment

Assessment advice

War Game is a novel that frames historical fact in a fictional storyline. You can use the novel to assess children's grasp of the way the author-illustrator has interwoven fact and fiction, both in the text and in the use of watercolour illustrations and contemporary print materials such as war posters. The fast-moving narrative follows the form of a chronological recount but it also demonstrates how a lucid, unembellished style can be an effective and moving narrative tool. Given the subject matter, there is considerable scope for linking into the history curriculum.

In the assessment activity below, the children are asked to compile a glossary of vocabulary relating to the First World War. You could also challenge the children to create their own assessment activities, for example, working in groups to devise multiple choice or true or false quizzes about the novel. They could devise spelling tests based on topics (landscape, weapons, military terms) or parts of speech (verbs, nouns, adjectives).

Great War glossary

Objective: To use syntax, context and word structure to build their store of vocabulary as they read for meaning.
What you need: Photocopiable page 32.

What to do

● Reflect with the children on what they have learned about the Great War (1914–18). Note key facts on the board under the journalistic headings: Who, What, When, Where and Why. Remind the children that this was called 'the war to end all wars' because it was so terrible and resulted in over 8 million deaths.

● Write one or two key technical terms on the board (trench warfare, the Front, No Man's Land) and challenge children to explain what they mean.

● Hand out photocopiable page 32 and explain that they are going to compile a glossary of technical terms used about the First World War.

● Let the children work on their own to complete the photocopiable sheet, using their knowledge of the novel. When they have finished, they should work with a writing partner, and compare their definitions, editing and improving them to contribute to a class glossary.

● Discuss what gaps the children have in their knowledge about the war, for example, ask: *How did the war end? What was the outcome of the war? In what ways did it change people's lives?* Help the children find suitable websites about the First World War and suggest research resources that can help them learn about the war, including contemporary photographs, film, letters, diaries and war poems. Encourage them to add more words to their glossary as they read more about the war.

● On the interactive whiteboard or computer, create a class glossary (in alphabetical order) for the First World War by gathering together the best definitions of words from the photocopiable sheet together with the new words that the children have suggested and defined from their research.

Great War glossary

- Explain the meaning of the following terms used in the novel.
- Add some new entries of your own.

The Front _____

No Man's Land _____

Morning hate _____

Communication trench _____

Pistol flare _____

Stand Down _____

Fire-step _____

Dugouts _____

Stand To _____

Shellfire _____

Parapet _____

Tommies _____

_____

_____